Boats

by Julie Murray

Visit us at www.abdopublishing.com

Published by Abdo Kids, a division of ABDO, PO Box 398166, Minneapolis, Minnesota 55439.

Copyright © 2015 by Abdo Consulting Group, Inc. International copyrights reserved in all countries.
No part of this book may be reproduced in any form without written permission from the publisher.

Printed in the United States of America, North Mankato, Minnesota.

032014

092014

 PRINTED ON RECYCLED PAPER

Photo Credits: Shutterstock, Thinkstock

Production Contributors: Teddy Borth, Jennie Forsberg, Grace Hansen

Design Contributors: Dorothy Toth, Laura Rask

Library of Congress Control Number: 2013953005

Cataloging-in-Publication Data

Murray, Julie.

 Boats / Julie Murray.

  p. cm. -- (Transportation)

ISBN 978-1-62970-078-6 (lib. bdg.)

Includes bibliographical references and index.

1. Boats--Juvenile literature.   I. Title.

623.82--dc23

2013953005

Table of Contents

Boats

Boats travel on water.

They are used on lakes,

rivers, and oceans.

4

Parts of a Boat

The body of a boat is called the **hull**. The front of a boat is the **bow**. The back is the **stern**.

bow

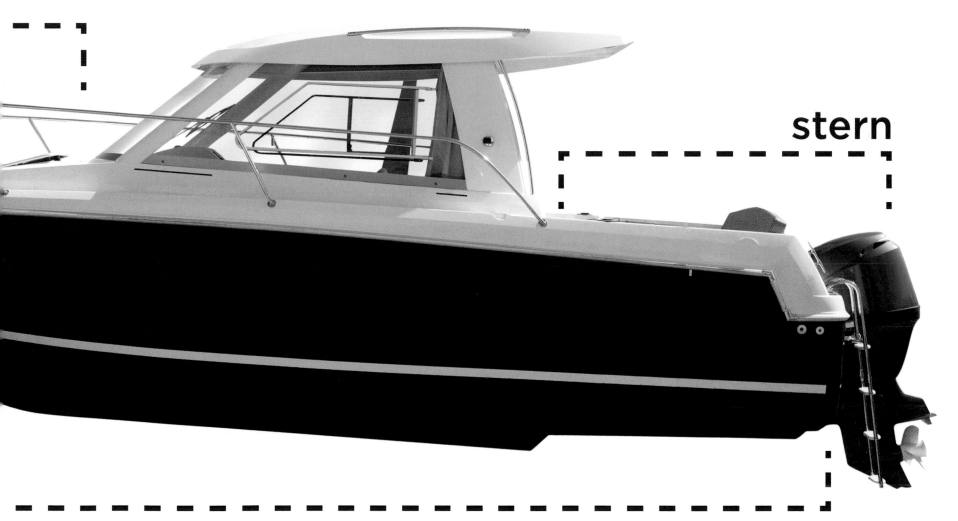

stern

hull

Different Kinds of Boats

There are many kinds of boats. Boats can be used for traveling, fishing, or just for fun.

9

Motorboats come in many sizes. They can be used for fishing, waterskiing, or cruising.

Big fishing boats use nets to catch fish. They can stay out at sea for weeks at a time.

Racing boats are made for speed. Some go as fast as 150 mph (240 km/h)!

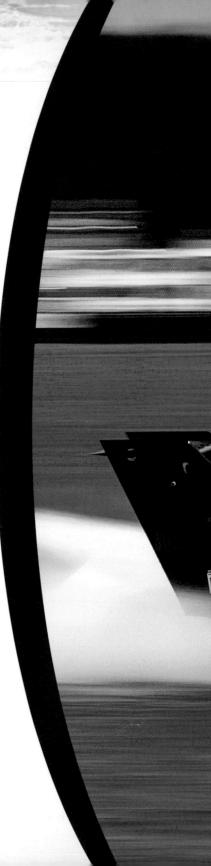

MATRIX SYSTEM
AUTOMOTIVE FINISHES

Mike Webster

MATRIX SYSTEM
AUTOMOTIVE FINISHES

MADISON FUDGE FACTORY

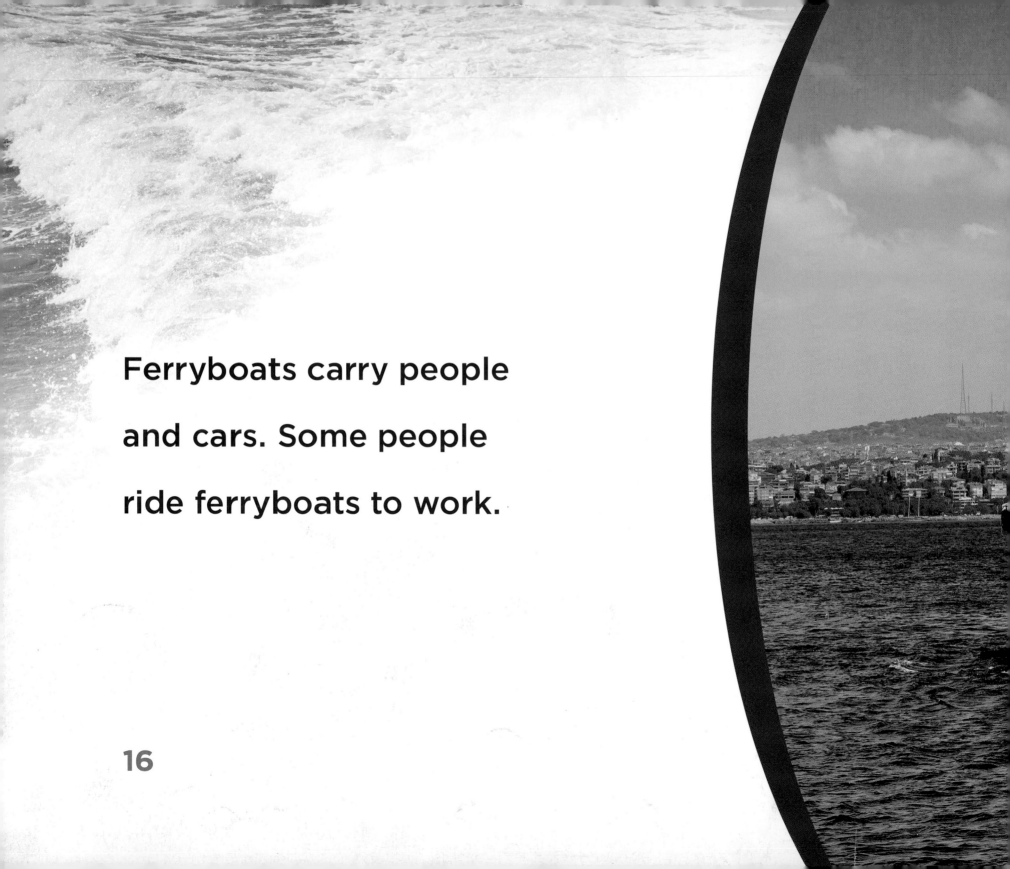

Ferryboats carry people and cars. Some people ride ferryboats to work.

17

Sailboats have big sails that catch the wind. Moving the **rudder** guides the boat.

19

Kayaks and canoes can be fun to use. **Paddles** are used to move these boats.

More Facts

- Australian Ken Warby set the record for fastest boat in 1978. His boat went over 350 mph (536 km/h)!

- Ken Warby's boat was named Spirit of Australia.

- The largest cruise ships are over 3 football fields long and can hold over 6,000 passengers!

- Today, it takes a modern ship about 6 to 7 days to cross the Atlantic Ocean. In 1819, the first steam-powered ship took about 30 days to make the same trip.

Glossary

bow – the front part of a ship.

hull – the part of the ship that floats in the water.

motorboat – a boat that is moved by a motor.

paddle – a long, flat, hand-held tool used to move the boat forward or in a different direction.

rudder – a blade at the stern of the boat that moves the boat in different directions.

stern – the back part of the ship.

Index

abdokids.com

Use this code to log on to abdokids.com and access crafts, games, videos and more!

Abdo Kids Code:
TBK0786